Simon Stephens a

Song from F:

C000244261

Bloomsbury Methuen Drama
An imprint of Bloomsbury Publishing Plc

B L O O M S B U R Y
LONDON • OXFORD • NEW YORK • NEW DELHI • SYDNEY

Bloomsbury Methuen Drama

An imprint of Bloomsbury Publishing Plc

www.bloomsbury.com

50 Bedford Square	1385 Broadway
London	New York
WC1B 3DP	NY 10018
UK	USA

BLOOMSBURY and the Diana logo
are trademarks of Bloomsbury Publishing Plc

First published 2015

British Library Cataloguing-in-Publication Data
A catalogue record for this book is available from the British Library

ISBN: PB: 978-1-4742-7735-8
ePub: 978-1-4742-7737-2
ePDF: 978-1-4742-7736-5

Library of Congress Cataloging-in-Publication Data
A catalog record for this book is available from the Library of Congress

Typeset by Country Setting, Kingsdown, Kent CT14 8ES
Printed and bound in Great Britain

Young Vic

Song from Far Away

by Simon Stephens and Mark Eitzel

Song from Far Away was first performed by Toneelgroep Amsterdam
at Mostra Internacional de Teatro de São Paulo, Brazil, on 10 March 2015.
This production opened at the Young Vic on 2 September 2015.

SONG FROM FAR AWAY

Text by **Simon Stephens**
Music and Lyrics by **Mark Eitzel**

A Toneelgroep Amsterdam production.
Mostra Internacional de Teatro de São Paulo, co-producer.
Young Vic: London co-producer.

Willem	**Eelco Smits**
Direction	**Ivo van Hove**
Design and Light	**Jan Versweyveld**
Dramaturgy	**Bart van den Eynde**
Assistant Designer	**Ramón Huijbrechts**

For Young Vic

Stage Manager	**Dan Gammon**
Lighting Operator	**Seb Barresi**
Sound Operator	**Amy Bramma**

For Toneelgroep Amsterdam

Private Producer	**Joachim Fleury**
Casting	**Hans Kemna**
Translation	**Rik van den Bos**
Head of Technical and Production	**Wolf-Götz Schwörer**
Production Leader	**Michiel van Schijndel**
First Stage Manager	**Sebastiaan Kruijs**
	Reyer Meeter
Stage Managers	**Erwin Sterk**
	Martijn Smolders
	Pepijn van Beek
	Emile Bleeker
	Peter Pieksma
	Pieter Roodbeen
	Ruud de Vos
	Zinzi Kemper
Head of Costume	**Wim van Vliet**
Costumes	**Farida Bouhbouh**
Publicity	**Mette Raaphorst**
Set Built By	**Kloosterboer Decor bv**

With generous support from The Richenthal Foundation,
the J. Paul Getty Jnr Charitable Trust
and the Embassy of the Kingdom of the Netherlands.

BIOGRAPHIES

Simon Stephens
Text

Simon is an Artistic Associate at the Lyric Hammersmith and a Literary Associate at the Royal Court.

Previous Young Vic: English-language versions of Anton Chekhov's *The Cherry Orchard*, Henrik Ibsen's *A Doll's House* (Young Vic, Duke of York's and BAM New York) and an adaptation of Jon Fosse's *I Am the Wind*.

Other theatre includes: *Heisenberg* (Manhattan Theatre Club, Broadway); *The Funfair* (adapted from Ödön von Horváth's *Kasimir and Karoline*, Home Theatre, Manchester); *Carmen Disruption* (Deutsches Schauspielhaus, Hamburg, and Almeida Theatre, London); *Birdland, Wastwater, Motortown, Country Music, Herons, Bluebird* (Royal Court); *The Curious Incident of the Dog in the Night-Time* (National Theatre, West End and Broadway); *Three Kingdoms* (NO99/Munich Playhouse/Lyric Hammersmith); *The Trial of Ubu* (Toneelgroep Amsterdam/ Hampstead); *T5, Heaven* (Traverse); *A Thousand Stars Explode in the Sky* (co-written with Robert Holman and David Eldridge, Lyric Hammersmith); *Marine Parade* (co-written with Mark Eitzel, Brighton Festival); *Punk Rock* (Lyric Hammersmith/Royal Exchange); *Seawall* (Bush/Traverse); *Harper Regan* (National Theatre); *Pornography* (Tricycle/Birmingham Rep/Edinburgh Festival/ Deutsches Schauspielhaus); *On the Shore of the Big Wide World* (Royal Exchange/ National Theatre); *Christmas* (Bush); *One Minute* (Crucible); and *Port* (Royal Exchange).

Television includes: *Cargese, Dive* and *Pornography.*

Mark Eitzel
Music and Lyrics

Mark Eitzel grew up in San Francisco, California, Taipei, Taiwan, and Southampton, UK. He has been a songwriter since 1980.

Albums written for American Music Club include: *Restless Stranger, Engine, California, United Kingdom, Everclear, Mercury, San Francisco, Love Songs for Patriots* and *The Golden Age.*

Solo work includes: *Songs of Love* (Live from the Borderline); *60 Watt Silver Lining, West* (written with Peter Buck from REM); *Caught in a Trap, The Invisible Man, Klamath* and *Don't Be a Stranger.*

His first collaboration with Simon Stephens was *Marine Parade*, which will have a revival in London in March 2016. He is currently working on a new album of music.

Ivo van Hove
Direction

Ivo has been general director of the Toneelgroep Amsterdam since 2001.

Toneelgroep Amsterdam includes: *Kings of War, Mary Stuart, The Fountainhead, Long Day's Journey into Night, Scenes from a Marriage, The Miser, Children of the Sun, Othello, Teorema, Summer Trilogy, Antonioni Project, Cries and Whispers, The Human Voice, Rocco and his Brothers, Angels in America* and *Roman Tragedies*.

Young Vic includes: *A View from the Bridge* (also West End and Broadway; Olivier Award for Best Direction).

Other theatre includes: *Antigone* (Barbican, Les Théâtres de la Ville de Luxembourg), *Strange Interlude, Ludwig II* (Munich Kammerspiele); *Edward II, The Misanthrope* (Schaubühne, Berlin); *Scenes from a Marriage, The Little Foxes, Hedda Gabler* (Obie Award), *A Streetcar Named Desire* (New York Theatre Workshop); *The Lady of the Camellias* and *The Miser* (Schauspielhaus, Hamburg).

Opera includes: *Brokeback Mountain* (Teatro Real, Madrid); *The Clemency of Titus* and *Idomeneo* (La Monnaie Opera, Brussels); *Mazeppa* (Komische Oper, Berlin); Verdi's *Macbeth* (L'Opera de Lyon); *Iolanta and The Makropulos Case* (De Nederlandse Opera); and *Lulu* and Wagner's *The Ring Cycle* (Flemish Opera).

Film and television includes: *Amsterdam* and *Home Front*.

Jan Versweyveld
Design and Light

Jan has been head of scenography and regular designer for Toneelgroep Amsterdam since 2001.

Toneelgroep Amsterdam includes: *Kings of War, Mary Stuart, The Fountainhead, Long Day's Journey into Night, Scenes from a Marriage, The Miser, Husbands, Children of the Sun, Theorem, Summer Trilogy, Antonioni Project, Cries and Whispers, The Human Voice, Rocco and his Brothers, Angels in America* and *Roman Tragedies*.

Young Vic includes: *A View from the Bridge* (also West End and Broadway).

Other theatre includes: *Antigone* (Barbican, Les Théâtres de la Ville de Luxembourg); *Strange Interlude, Ludwig II* (Munich Kammerspiele); *Edward II, The Misanthrope* (Schaubühne, Berlin); *Scenes from a Marriage* (Lucille Lortel Award for Outstanding Scenic Design); *The Little Foxes, Hedda Gabler* (Obie Award), *A Streetcar Named Desire* (New York Theatre Workshop); *The Lady of the Camellias* and *The Miser* (Schauspielhaus, Hamburg).

Opera includes: *Brokeback Mountain, Boris Godunov* (Teatro Real, Madrid); *The Clemency of Titus, Idomeneo King of Crete* (La Monnaie Opera, Brussels); *Mazeppa* (Komische Oper, Berlin); Verdi's *Macbeth* (L'Opera de Lyon); *Iolanta, The Makropulos Case* (De Nederlandse Opera); and *Lulu* and Wagner's *The Ring Cycle* (Flemish Opera).

Dance includes: *Rain, Love Supreme, Small Hands, Just Before* and *Drumming* (Rosas).

Bart van den Eynde
Dramaturgy

Young Vic includes: *A View from the Bridge.*

Other theatre includes: *Antonioni Project, Roman Tragedies, Scenes from a Marriage, The Massacre at Paris* (Toneelgroep Amsterdam); *Parsifal, Cyrano, Headbanger's Wall* (NTGent); *Terminator Trilogy* (FC Bergman); *The Institute for Recently Extinct Species* (Kunstenfestivaldesarts); *Edward II* (Schaubühne, Berlin); *The Miser, Hedda Gabler, Alice in Bed, A Streetcar Named Desire* and *More Stately Mansions* (New York Theatre Workshop).

Dance includes: *Built to Last, Do Animals Cry, All Together Now, Blessed, It's Not Funny* (Damaged Goods); *1001, i!2* (Kobalt Works); *Primero* (Les Ballets C de la B); and *Forever Overhead* (Voetvolk).

Performance includes: *Mommy, Daddy, Me* (Veridiana Zurita); *A Possibility of an Abstraction* and *Carry On* (Germaine Kruip).

Eelco Smits
Willem

Eelco has been a member of Toneelgroep Amsterdam since 2005.

Theatre for Toneelgroep Amsterdam includes: *Kings of War, Angels in America, Phaedra, Ghosts, Antonioni Project, Teorema, Roman Tragedies, Summer Trilogy, The Taming of the Shrew, Tartuffe, The Seagull, Mourning Becomes Electra, Opening Night, The Russians!, The Miser, Nora, Hamlet vs. Hamlet* and *Mary Stuart.*

Other theatre includes: *Leonce and Lena, Portia Coughlan* and *Op zoek naar de verloren tijd* (Ro Theater).

Film and television includes: *Bloedverwanten, Moordvrouw, Lijn 32, Van God Los* and *Majesteit.*

The Cut Bar and Restaurant
Our bar and restaurant is a relaxing place to meet and eat. An inspired mix of classic and original play-themed dishes made from fresh, free-range and organic ingredients creates an exciting menu.

www.thecutbar.com

The Young Vic is a company limited by guarantee, registered in England No. 1188209

VAT registration No. 236 673 348

The Young Vic (registered charity No 268876) received public funding from

Our shows
We present the widest variety of classics, new plays, forgotten works and music theatre. We tour and co-produce extensively within the UK and internationally.

Our artists
Our shows are created by some of the world's great theatre people alongside the most adventurous of the younger generation. This fusion makes the Young Vic one of the most exciting theatres in the world.

Our audience
. . . is famously the youngest and most diverse in London. We encourage those who don't think theatre is 'for them' to make it part of their lives. We give 10 per cent of our tickets to schools and neighbours irrespective of box-office demand, and keep prices low.

Our partners near at hand
Each year we engage with 10,000 local people – individuals and groups of all kinds including schools and colleges – by exploring theatre on and off stage. From time to time we invite our neighbours to appear on our stage alongside professionals.

Our partners further away
By co-producing with leading theatre, opera and dance companies from London and around the world we create shows neither partner could achieve alone.

markit
Lead sponsor of the Young Vic's funded ticket scheme

Get more from the Young Vic online

Sign up to receive email updates at youngvic.org/register

 youngvictheatre

 @youngvictheatre

 youngviclondon

 youngviclondon.wordpress.com

 @youngvictheatre

THE YOUNG VIC COMPANY

Artistic Director
David Lan
Executive Director
Lucy Woollatt

Associate Artistic
Director
Sue Emmas
Lead Producer
Daisy Heath
General Manager/
Producer
Ben Cooper

Genesis Fellow
Gbolahan Obisesan

ASSOCIATES
Associate Designer
Jeremy Herbert
Associate Artists
Joe Hill-Gibbins
Julia Horan
Ian MacNeil
Sacha Wares
International Associates
Benedict Andrews
Luc Bondy
Gísli Örn Gardarsson
Amir Nizar Zuabi
Associate Companies
1927
Belarus Free Theatre
BirdGang
**Regional Theatre Young
Directors Scheme**

ADMINISTRATION
Assistant Producer
Iain Goosey
Administration Manager
Nastasia Tryphonos
Database Administrator
Lee-Anne Inglis
Administrator to the
Producers
Claire Turner

Assistant to the Artistic
Director
Andrew Hughes

DEVELOPMENT
Director of Development
& Commercial
Investment
and MD Young Vic films
Alan Stacey
Trusts Fundraising
Manager
Livvy Brinson
Development Manager
Sandy McKay
Lisa Morlidge

Research Officer
Natasha Ratter
Development Assistant
Vanessa Onwuemezi

FINANCE
Finance Manager
Sophie Wells
Finance and
Contracts Assistant
Janine Carter

FRONT OF HOUSE
Theatre Manager
Paul Marshall
Front of House Manager
Will Bowden
Operations Assistant
Frank Osborne
Duty Managers
Mike Beigel
Megan Griffith
Matt Hatt
Ushers
Yolanda Aladeshelu
Simone Bell
Omari Biriye
Clair Burningham
Debbie Burningham
Ali Burton
Oliver Byng
Joseph Cocklin
Laura Day
Francesca De Sica
Eboni Dixon
Sile Edwards
Lynne Egwuekwe
Patrick Elue
Kayode Ewumi
Lee Flynn
Tom Handril
Susan Harrold
Owen Haselgrave
Shermin Hassan
William Heslop
Jim Hutcheson
Nicole Jacobs
Toheeb Jimoh
Grace Kayibanda
Aaron Kelly
Lynn Knight
Radi Kopacki
George Mills
Glenn Mortimer
Taz Munyaneza
Sheila Murphy
Ciarra Nevitt
Tobi Oludipe
Nadine Paquette
Julie Patten
Mariko Primarolo
**Gracjana Rejmer-
Canovas**
Imogen Robertson
Nathan Rumney
Thea Sandall
Zeni Sekabanja
Joanna Selcott

Paula Shaw
Lara Simpson
Joe Skelton
Mark Vanderstoop
Isaac Vincent
Eve Williams
Dan Young

MARKETING AND
PRESS
Director of Marketing
and Press
Stacy Coyne
Press Manager
Charlotte Bayley
Ticketing Manager
James Orr
Marketing Officer
Aurora Lewis
Marketing Assistant
Leonara Manyangadze
Press and Publications
Assistant
Priya Roy

PRODUCTION
Technical Director
Igor
Production Manager
Bernd Fauler
Company Manager
Anna Cole
Head of Sound
Alex Twiselton
Head of Lighting
Nicki Brown
Head of Stage
Simon Evans
Head of Costume
Catherine Kodicek
Workshop Manager
Emma Hayward
Senior Stage Technician
Hilary Williamson
Senior Sound Technician
Amy Bramma
Senior Lighting
Technician
Nicole Smith
Stage Technician
Nick Aldrich
Production Manager
(Studios)
Neil Mickel
Production
Administrator
Hannah Falvey
Sound Apprentice
April Danbrook

TAKING PART
Director of Taking Part
Imogen Brodie
Participation Project
Manager
Sharon Kanolik
Two Boroughs Project
Manager
Lily Einhorn

Schools and Colleges
Project Manager
(maternity cover)
Rob Lehmann
Two Boroughs &
Directors
Programme Project
Manager
Kirsten Adam
Taking Part and
Administration Assistant
Daniel Harrison

WELCOME TEAM
Welcome Team Manager
Ciara O'Toole
Welcome Team
Liz Arday
Joshua Coppi
Johanna Keane
Rosa Manzi Reid
Boris Van Der Ree
Niall Wilson

BOARD
Patrick McKenna
(Chair)
Sean Egan
David Fletcher
Sarah Hall
Patrick Handley
Clive Jones
Rory Kinnear
Carol Lake
David Lan
Anna Lane
Ivan Lewis MP
Karen McHugh
Rita Skinner
Jane Storie
Steve Tompkins
Bill Winters

DEVELOPMENT
BOARD
Rotha Bell
Beatrice Bondy
Caroline Cormack
Anna Lane
Jill Manson
Will Meldrum
Chris Organ
Barbara Reeves
Mark Selby
Rita Skinner
Bill Winters

ON LEAVE
Associate Director
Natalie Abrahami
Front of House Manager
(maternity leave)
Claire Harris
Schools and Colleges
Project Manager
(maternity leave)
Georgia Dale

SUPPORTING THE YOUNG VIC

The Young Vic relies on the generous support of many individuals, trusts, foundations, and companies to produce our work, on and off stage. For their recent support we thank

Public Funders
Arts Council England
British Council
Creative & Cultural Skills
Lambeth Borough Council
Southwark Council

Corporate Partners
Barclays
Berkeley Group
Bloomberg
Edelman
Markit
Wahaca

Corporate Members
aka
Bloomberg
Clifford Chance
Edelman
Ingenious Media PLC
Mishcon de Reya
Royal Bank of Scotland
  and NatWest
Wisdom Council

Partners and Upper Circle
David and Corinne Abbott
Tony & Gisela Bloom
Daniel Friel
Patrick Handley
Jack & Linda Keenan
Chris & Jane Lucas
Patrick McKenna
Simon & Midge Palley
Karl-Johan Persson
Jon & NoraLee Sedmak
Dasha Shenkman
Rita & Paul Skinner
Bruno Wang
Anda & Bill Winters

Soul Mates
Jane Attias
Chris & Frances Bates
Anthony & Karen Beare
Joanne Beckett
Royce & Rotha Bell
Guy America &
  Dominique Bellec
The Bickertons
Sarah Billinghurst Solomon
Lisa and Adrian Banks
Beatrice Bondy
Katie Bradford
CJ & LM Braithwaite
Kay Ellen Consolver
Caroline & Ian Cormack
Lucy & Spencer de Grey

Annabel Duncan-Smith
Sean Egan
Jennifer & Jeff Eldredge
Don Ellwood & Sandra Johnigan
Paul Gambaccini
Sarah Gay Fletcher
Jill and Jack Gerber
Rory Godson
Annika Goodwille
Manfred and Lydia Gorvy
Sarah Hall
Richard Hardman & Family
Madeleine Hodgkin
Nik Holttum & Helen Brannigan
Jane Horrocks
Linden Ife
Maxine Isaacs
Clive Jones
Tom Keatinge
John Kinder & Gerry Downey
Carol Lake
Martha Lane Fox
Jude Law
Tony Mackintosh
James & Sue Macmillan
Jill & Justin Manson
Karen McHugh
Ian McKellen
Barbara Minto
Miles Morland
Georgia Oetker
Powerscourt
Rob & Lesley O'Rahilly
Barbara Reeves
Anthony & Sally Salz
Catherine Schreiber
Carol Sellars
Justin Shinebourne
Olga Slater
Nicola Stanhope
Sir Patrick Stewart
Eva Boenders & Scott Stevens
Jan & Michael Topham
Totally Theatre Productions
The Ulrich Family
Donna & Richard Vinter
Jimmy & Carol Walker
Rob Wallace
Edgar & Judith Wallner

Trust Supporters
95.8 Capital FM's
  Help a Capital Child
Amberstone Trust
Andor Charitable Trust
Austin & Hope Pilkington Trust
BBC Children in Need
Backstage Trust
Boris Karloff Charitable
  Foundation

Boshier Hinton Foundation
The City Bridge Trust
The Cleopatra Trust
Clifford Chance Foundation
Clore Duffield Foundation
Cockayne – Grants for the Arts
John S Cohen Foundation
The Cooperative Membership
  Community Fund
The Creative Employment
  Programme
David Laing Foundation
The Dr. Mortimer and
  Theresa Sackler Foundation
D'Oyly Carte Charitable Trust
Embassy of the Kingdom
  of the Netherlands
Equitable Charitable Trust
The Eranda Foundation
Ernest Cook Trust
The Foyle Foundation
Garfield Weston Foundation
Garrick Charitable Trust
Genesis Foundation
Golden Bottle Trust
Golsoncott Foundation
The Harold Hyam Wingate
  Foundation
Jerwood Charitable Foundation
Joanies Fund
John Ellerman Foundation
John Thaw Foundation
J. Paul Getty Jnr
  Charitable Trust
The Kidron and Hall Family
The Limbourne Trust
The London Community
  Foundation
The Mackintosh Foundation
Martin Bowley Charitable Trust
Mrs Margaret Guido's
  Charitable Trust
Newcomen Collett Foundation
The Noel Coward Foundation
The Nomura Charitable Trust
The Portrack Charitable Trust
The Rayne Trust
The Red Hill Trust
Richard Radcliffe
  Charitable Trust
The Richenthal Foundation
Royal Norwegian Embassy
The Sackler Trust
Sir Walter St John's
  Educational Charity
The Wolfson Foundation

*and all other donors who wish
to remain anonymous.*

toneelgroepamsterdam

Toneelgroep Amsterdam (TA) is one of the leading ambassadors of Dutch performing art in the Netherlands and abroad, with a core composed of a broad and highly versatile ensemble of world famous actors and a team of leading directors. Well-known productions include *Angels in America, Roman Tragedies, Opening Night, The Fountainhead* and *Kings of War*.

TA is the in-house company of Amsterdam's Stadsschouwburg Theatre and performs on stages worldwide. TA has been invited by international festivals such as RuhrTriennale, Wiener Festwochen, the Edinburgh Festival and Festival d'Avignon, and performs in the United States, Russia and Australia.

TA is led by Ivo van Hove, who has been instrumental in attracting sensational international directors to the group such as Thomas Ostermeier, Krzysztof Warlikowski, Grzegorz Jarzyna, Luk Perceval, Simon Stone, Guy Cassiers and Sam Gold, as well as members of a new generation directing talent.

TA sets itself apart by staging innovative and contemporary productions from the classic and modern repertoire for a wide audience in the Netherlands and abroad. The group performs for around 110,000 people a year, helping ensure that repertory theatre remains an indispensable component of contemporary culture.

TA has an extensive talent development programme in areas such as acting, directing and stage design, as well as theatre technology and back-office work. In addition, TA has an extensive education programme, including an annual junior production, and there is a programme of other events occurring almost every day under the title of TA-extra. Furthermore, TA works together with alliance partners Adelheid|Female Economy and De Warme Winkel.

markit

Markit is proud to be the Lead Sponsor of the

Young Vic's Funded Ticket Programme

Enabling theatre to be enjoyed by all

markit.com

Song from Far Away

Characters

Willem, *thirty-four years old*

January 25th

Dear Pauli

I was in a meeting in an office on Franklin and Church Street when Mum called. I seem to always work on Sundays nowadays. A Chinese girl with a surprisingly quiet voice was trying to sell me the idea of corn-based investments in the farmlands of central America over the next thirty years. I was trying my hardest to listen to her and to not get obsessed with how quiet her voice was. It helped if I imagined I was talking to her on Skype. I was embarrassed on her behalf because she'd not done her research and I knew about four times as much about the future of corn markets in central America as she did. I was on the cusp of asking her to stop talking and correcting the errors in her data because her data was simply out of date when Mum's call came through.

The Chinese girl partly looked furious that I'd not turned my phone off and partly looked like she knew it was inevitable that I wouldn't, but, hey, at least I didn't answer it. But then after the ringing died away I looked at her expecting her to carry on as though nothing had happened, and she didn't.

She stopped talking.
She was staring at me.

She had a look on her face that was like she knew something awful had happened. Something more than just the embarrassment of a phone call interrupting a sales meeting. Something unspeakably bad. The voicemail alert sound came through, and then a text message.

You live a day. You get up. You get a coffee. You don't have time for breakfast at home so you get some kind of banana-based yoghurt thing at a deli on the corner of Chambers Street and Church from a guy with what can only be described as a broken eye socket and the winter sun is rising over the Hudson and every single boy is looking glorious in the freezing morning air and the world smells of coffee and

mint and leather and New York is afrost with glory and you
go to your office and the office is kind of clicking and you take
a car to your meeting and Oscar's on the Sunday shift and he
kind of knows you've got a thing about him and he's married
but he always flashes a smile and the meeting's underwhelming
but the Chinese girl's weird voice and uncanny facial expression
is as fascinating as it is irritating and then a voicemail message
comes crashing in from the other side of the world and
everything changes.

Mum's voice on the phone had the hollow blankness that you
can only get if you've seen something you should never have
seen.

She told me that I had to come home. She told me what had
happened to you. She told me that it would be Wednesday.
She told me that you would be going to Zorgvlied.

I have to say it came at a very inconvenient time. The phone
call. So when I rang her back I was short with her.

Oscar drove me back to my apartment and waited outside
while I packed my case. I was going to ask him to come in.
I didn't.

I clamped my headphones down over my ears as I headed
to security to drown out the sound of the world but I wasn't
playing any music because I never play music so that all I
could hear was my own breathing.

Breathe in.
Breathe out.
Breath in.
Breathe out.

I entered the lounge by invitation only. It felt like I could live
there for the rest of my life. I could sleep there easily. I could
eat their food for years and years. The beautifully made
sandwiches and the fresh dim sum and the tiny cupcakes.
Drink their Hendrick's with ice and cucumber. Have a
massage every morning.

Enjoy the silence and the stillness of the air. Nobody ever notices you in places like that.

Evening was falling as I got my place on the plane. I avoided all eye-contact with the people who shuffled past me to the cheap seats. And stared out the window. The airport was red. The whole world sounded like it was humming.

I drank three glasses of Scotch and ginger ale before we'd even cleared Coney Island. The stewardess had that look on her face. 'I see. We've got a live one here.' In business class the cabin crew like a drinker. They recognise a fellow nomad when they see one. I fell asleep as the plane cut away from the East Coast and headed out over the Atlantic.

When I woke up there was a woman crouching next to me. I have no idea where she came from or what she was doing there. She was about seventy years old. She woke me up to tell me she was sorry. She held my hand. Her hand was like a little claw. Her finger bones cold beneath her skin. She asked me what day the funeral was. She had a way of speaking that was like she was trying not to laugh. I told her Wednesday without even thinking. 'How did you know I was going back for a funeral?' She smiled like she couldn't hear me because she was old and deaf and she didn't say another word. She stood up and walked away. I looked to see where she went but I couldn't find her anywhere.

It was then that I decided to write you these letters.

I decided to try to call Isaac when I land. I've not seen Isaac since I came to New York. I've not seen him, in fact, since I left him. There was something about returning this time that made me very much want to see him again.

There's always a moment as the plane pulls in to land when I know with certainty that we'll crash on impact and the whole roaring tube of metal and oil will scream into fire and noise. We don't. The landing is perfectly smooth.

I imagine the captain, crisp, white shirt, beautiful retro Ray-Bans, giving his co-pilot a resonant high five.

Ladies and gentlemen, welcome to Amsterdam.

January 26th

Dear Pauli

Schiphol isn't an airport any more. It used to be. In the sixties. Nowadays Schiphol is a small suburb. It took me forty-five minutes to reach the smoking lounge at Murphy's Bar. I got there and it seemed like the only real place left in the world.

I drank a Scotch and ginger ale and then a bitter double espresso, smoked three American Spirit and tried to readjust my body clock. It was eleven-thirty in the morning.

Dad called me the second I left the place.

I had the best idea. It made perfect sense. I told Dad that I wasn't going to stay at home. I told him the bank had offered to hire me a room at the Lloyd Hotel. I was going to take them up on their offer. It made much more sense. Where would I sleep if I stayed with them? I'd have to sleep in your room. I'd go round later but I needed rest.

I could picture him speaking as he tried to control his anger. His voice clipped off in the middle of a word. 'If that's what you want.'

I've always loved the Lloyd. A hundred years ago they built this building for emigrants to stay while they waited for their boats to take them to the New World. The place of embarkation.

The lobby at the Lloyd was bright from the winter morning sunshine. All tiled and wooden and echoing like a cruiser. The man on the desk was small and elegant and somebody came to take my bags up to my room. I tipped him ten euros.

The water in the shower was strong and it was warm and it felt for a second that it was strong enough to pour through my skin and clean out my insides and the soap smelt of lemongrass and for a while I forgot what I was even doing here.

I called down to reception to bring me a sandwich and a beer. The shower and the sandwich almost brought me back to life.

I couldn't face Mum and Dad. I rang Dad. I told him I was exhausted, and told him that my plan was to sleep all day. The way he pronounced the word 'disappointment' made it sound like a toxin. I could hear him biting his tongue as he asked me to go round tomorrow, they were going to the doctor's for the results of your post-mortem and I promised I would.

And I went out. I went for a walk.

I decided I was going to walk the whole span of Herengracht. I crossed over at Brouwersgracht to walk in the cold back round Singel Home to Damstraat. It was the kind of cold that sits in your bones. The sky was a thick grey.

The water made things quieter, made me realise that none of this is real.

The city was a chorus of rattling trams and bewildering underwear billboard posters and cafés and railings shuttering off unfinished building work and unpredictable self-satisfied cyclists who rode with the anger of those convinced they will save the world.

It was five in the afternoon by the time I got to Reguliersdwars-straat. It hasn't changed. Gay bars never change. I decided I was going to drink a cocktail. I deserved a cocktail. It was the least I could do.

I went to Dvars. I ordered a White Russian and sent Isaac a text and silently I drank your health. There was a tune playing in the bar. And there was a phrase in the melody that caught my heart in its hand. I tried to memorise it.

'Isaac. This is Willem. I'm in Amsterdam. I don't know if you heard, Pauli died last week. It was very sudden. He had a heart attack. The doctors don't know what caused it. The funeral's on Wednesday. It'd be good to see you if you're around.' How could anybody refuse?

I waited to see if he replied straight away.

I was thinking about ordering another drink when this man came and sat opposite me. He told me his name was Marcello. He told me he was Brazilian. He told me that he spoke five languages. He worked as a call centre operative for a Brazilian IT company and he was in Amsterdam to buy a guitar. He told me he was a collector of guitars. He came to Amsterdam because he liked the idea of buying a musical instrument in every major city in Europe. He asked me what job I did. I didn't tell him.

I bought him a drink instead.

Isaac didn't text.

These are some of the things Marcello told me. I thought they'd make you smile. He told me he didn't understand the human race. The problem with the human race, he said, was that people are always throwing babies in dumpsters. Why are they doing that? People are always throwing babies in dumpsters. He repeated it over and over.

He told me he liked the stars. He was sad because he couldn't see the stars in the winter sky in Amsterdam. He said the stars lead us with strings around our throats towards the edge of the cliff and he always enjoyed watching that. He told me about his medication. He told me he liked my hands. He told me he wanted to watch me sleep.

We had five drinks together. The elegant man on the reception at the Lloyd welcomed me back and didn't bat an eye as Marcello held my hand and we walked up the stairs.

I remember when you were about twelve years old. You'd been having, I don't know, a problem at school or something. Some nonsense with a teacher or with something or other and you were finding it all very, very difficult to cope with. You said to me that everybody was always telling you that it was worth it in the end. Everybody was always telling you that if you did the work then, when you were twelve, then, in the end you'd be grateful for it.

You told me it felt like you were on this miserable train journey where you had to work hard and endure misery because when you got to where the train was going then everything would make sense. But what if there was no end? What if all there was was this journey and everybody was on this journey and everybody thought they were heading towards something and they were enduring misery and nonsense and bullshit and horror now because in the end they'd be glad they put up with it all. But what if the train just kept going for ever and ever?

I remember thinking that most twelve-year-olds didn't speak like that.

Afterwards I lay with my head on Marcello's chest. I could hear his voice echo around his torso. He was talking to me about the element of carbon. The element of carbon is the prerequisite for every form of life. It is the source of all organic things. When a body is burned or when a body decomposes in a grave, in time it is reduced to the element of carbon. We go back to the beginning.

He told me I could sleep. He'd watch me.
He told me it had started to snow.

January 27th

Dear Pauli

He didn't rob me. You'll laugh when I tell you it was the first thing I checked when I woke up in the morning. He noticed me check for it. It was excruciating for both of us. I asked him to come and have breakfast with me but he told me he wouldn't.

I wanted to say to him: 'Why don't we knock this whole fucking funeral business on the head? Why don't you take me back home with you to São Paulo? I want more than anything I've wanted for you to take me back to São Paulo?' I didn't say any of this.

He held the back of my neck and kissed my cheek. It was a good night, wasn't it? Sometimes that's enough. He told me he'd friend me on Facebook.

When I was having my breakfast Isaac texted me. He can't make it to the funeral. He has to work. He asked me if I wanted to see him on Friday before I went back to New York.

You know what's annoying? My brother died. I'm going to have to get used to saying that sentence out loud. My brother died last week. My brother died last month. My brother died last year. My brother died when I was thirty-four.

I decided to walk to Mum and Dad's because it would take a lot longer and I wanted it to take as long as it possibly could. I didn't want to come home. Dancing my way through the tourists and the teenagers and the Turkish men offering to repair my telephone.

I concentrated on my breathing as I waltzed through the old town. Trying not to slip on the cobbles by the canal.
Headphones clamped.
Breathe in.
Breathe out.
Breathe in.
Breathe out.

The windows were shining this morning. They were shining in the snow. It struck me this morning that the windows in this city aren't there just so that people can look out of them. The windows in this city are there to demonstrate to the world just how civilised we are. The windows in this city are designed to shove the worlds of our homes down the throats of everyone who comes here. So we can never leave.

And everything here is beautiful. And everything here is fine. Our tolerance shines like the snow in our windows and the warmth and the beauty of our interior designs and the generosity of the fruit in our fruit bowls. We can shove the fucking Africans and the Turks and the Surinamese out into Slotervaart and then congratulate ourselves with how tolerant we are and go and have another waffle.

Mum's face when she saw me. In spite of everything her eyes lit up.

Dad asked me how the Lloyd was. He's been made head of faculty. The senior otolaryngologist, he said. The ear and throat doctor of the Low Countries. He had no idea what to say to me so he talked to me about his work.

Mum went to make me an omelette.

When he was left alone with me he kept looking behind him and slightly to his right. As though he was nervous there was somebody there. He told me that if he were being honest with me I'd let him down. I'd let my mum down. There are some things, he told me, that you just don't do. He spoke very quietly so that Mum didn't hear. To watch him move so nervously and talk so quietly while he said things to leave me feeling like shit was just fascinating.

'Your sister's here,' he said. 'She's in the kitchen.' He said it like it was a gift.

And she was there. Mina. She was emptying the dishwasher. Putting all of the plates back in the precisely right cupboards. Correcting the stacks and the rows as she went. She gave me a little shy smile. She said sorry. She said she just wanted things to be tidy for Mum and Dad. She's tidied things away all her life, Pauli, it has nothing whatsoever to do with Mum and Dad. We went to kiss each other but we got it all wrong

and we kind of bumped ears with each other and that was
a bit funny and a bit sad. Anka and Henrick were at school.
I'll see them tomorrow.

People keep bringing food. Mum got really angry about it.
She can still cook food. She's not completely collapsed. She's
not climbed into a hole in the wall and disappeared.

Mina said a lot of your friends would be there tomorrow.
Young people. I don't know how much patience I've got for
sobbing twenty-year-olds right now. Some of them might be
quite cute.

I played your guitar. I figured out that tune that I heard at
Dvars.

Dr Siriwardena smiled at us when we went into his room.
He had to get an extra chair for Mina, and I stood up. He
hadn't been anticipating four of us. The way he smiled felt
downright rude. I thought for a second Mum was going to
ask him what the fuck he thought he was smiling about. Dad
seemed at home. Like the shape of the room and the certificates
on the wall and the books on his shelves made him feel like
he knew where he was all of a sudden.

Dr Siriwardena told us he was sorry for our loss.

So. Pauli. It seems that you had something called an inherited
carotid artery disease. There was something wrong with your
heart. Nobody noticed until it was too late. The likelihood is
that Dad's got it too. And he would have inherited it from his
dad. Sometimes it can go for generations without affecting
people. Sometimes they die of other things first so it doesn't
get diagnosed. Dr Siriwardena told Dad that he should get
himself checked out. If he's diagnosed with the same thing
it's very possible to treat it. He can prescribe some pills.
Normally he's made aware of the illness in children when
their parents are affected. Sometimes it goes backwards. It's
unusual. But not exceptional.

You should have seen Dad's face when he heard that, Pauli.

You saved his life. I've never seen a human face dissolve like that. It was like his face was made of sand.

I should get myself checked out too. You're whispering in our ear. Telling us to look after our hearts.

The same thing could happen to me, Pauli. I could fall down dead on Park Avenue outside a branch of fucking Wells Fargo and have all the strangers that surround me try to support my head. You weren't even with any of your friends, Pauli. You were on your own. There was a woman there. She rested your head in her lap. She said she knew straight away what had happened. She stroked your hair. She was talking to you. I dread to think what sentimental nonsense she'd come up with. I wonder if you heard what she said.

We exist in the gaps between the sounds that we make.
We all die interrupted.
And you've got no more sounds left, Pauli. You've disappeared without trace.

Dad dropped Mina home.

I cooked some pasta and heated up some sauce that Mum's next-door neighbour had brought over.

When I was cooking I could hear Dad in the room next door. He was crying. He made these big old loud sobs. I'd never heard anything like them.

He went to bed after we'd eaten and I sat up with Mum.

We drank two bottles of Chenin Blanc. She told me about the unusual amount of cleaning Mina had been doing around the house. For the past week it's been like she couldn't stop herself. She said she'd never seen Dad cry like this in all the time they'd been together.

She looked at me for a long time without saying anything. She could see into my future. She knew I would have days like hers.

I'm fucking angry with you, Pauli, can I tell you? You fucking selfish shit. Doing this to me. Making me come back here. Making me reheat frozen pasta sauce. Making me look at Mum while she gazed at me like that. Making me check I'd brought my cigarette butts in from outside. One stray cigarette butt left in the flower beds and Mina would have a breakdown. Making me watch Dad's jerking stiffness as he tried to control his fury and hid in his room and sobbed like a wounded dog. That's your fault, Pauli. I blame nobody but you. And tomorrow? The shit you're going to put me through, tomorrow? You should apologise, Pauli. You really should, you – You should.

I came back to my room. Everybody else was in bed. Everybody in this whole fucking city goes to bed early. It's like we're trying to shame the tourists by showing them how civilised we can be.

I took my shoes off. I took my jacket off. Hung my suit up. Hung my clothes in the closet. Stared in the mirror for a long time trying not to see the ghosts of Dad's face in the shape of my jawbone and the folds of my skin. Turned on the television. Turned off the television.

Put my pants and my socks into the side pocket of my suitcase ready to wash them when I got back to New York.

Sat at my desk. Got the hotel notepaper out. I tried two different pencils before settling on this one.

January 28th

Dear Pauli

Pauli, my friend, there were hundreds and hundreds of people there. Some of them recognised me and some of them didn't and some of them looked heartbroken and some of them looked beautiful and some of them were happy to see each other and just chatting nicely and some of them were crying their hearts out and some of them were looking brave and some of them were chuckling as though they'd said something inappropriate and secretly enjoyed saying it and some of them looked awkward because they didn't know anybody else and some of them weren't wearing black clothes so they felt a bit out of place and some of them were singing a sad little song but I couldn't hear them clearly enough to know what it was. I watched them as they left the church. For one moment it felt like everything was happening in the present tense.

They lowered your body into the ground, Pauli. It was fascinating. It seemed very efficient. It seemed functional. It looked lower than I'd thought six feet would have done. The soil on the ground was cold. The idea of that amount of soil on top of you. Hundreds and hundreds and hundreds of kilograms. And the stones and the wood and the metal and the leaves and the snow.

A few people came home, back to the house afterwards. Uncle Michiel was there. He kept smiling. It was like he was smiling so widely because he was trying to cheer everybody up.

He told me about all the countries in South America people would go to after they'd first left the Lloyd Hotel. He told me about the journey across the Atlantic and the route the boats would take. He told me about the political history of Suriname. I asked him if he'd ever been to South America. He smiled. Said of course he hadn't. The furthest he'd ever been was Paris.

He asked me if I wanted to buy some rugs. He'd bought some rugs from a man in Rotterdam. Real Persian rugs from Iran. I could have them for 60 per cent of the normal retail price. I'd be able to sell them on, easily. I told him I was fine for rugs. He told me that if I changed my mind I only needed to talk to him.

'Life's sad, Willem. Life's crazy. If I've learned anything in my life it's that it has no meaning or no purpose. But sometimes it is fascinating.'

Everybody left by about six o'clock. I called Isaac. I shouldn't have done that. He answered. I felt like a schoolkid all of a sudden.

He talked as though he was thinking about something else. I think he was online. He asked me how I was. He asked me how Mum and Dad were. He told me to tell them how sorry he was. He told me he'd seen you a few months ago. In the background, in the room he was in, it was like there was a radio or something and it was playing that song I'd heard in Dvars.

Mum asked me to stay the night. She asked me to stay in your room. She asked me to get Dad into bed. He'd been drinking since ten o'clock in the morning. He couldn't speak. He was sitting in the living room staring at the television, which wasn't turned on, and listening to something very quiet on the radio. He only noticed me when I turned the radio off.

'I was listening to that.'

He was slurring his words. He could barely open his mouth.

'Don't tell me to go to bed. Who do you think you are? How dare you come round here telling me what I should or shouldn't do? How dare you do that? How dare you? How dare you? How dare you? How dare you?'

I couldn't sleep.

I stayed up all night watching the shadows in your room change. They got more defined as the sun rose. The colours on all of the things in your room got sharper in the morning light. The books on your shelves and your CDs and your clothes and your posters on your wall came into focus. Your room was exactly as you'd left it, Pauli. Your sock drawer was left open. A towel left draping over your radiator.

January 29th

Dear Pauli

Mum wanted to have a meal with the family before I went back to New York. She invited Mina to come back round with Anka and Henrick. She invited Uncle Michiel.

I helped her clean the house. I helped her make breakfast for Dad. I talked to him. He didn't remember anything he'd said to me last night.

I went out to get some wine and some bread for the soup Mum made. Stopped and had a quick beer in a bar in Hobbemastraat. Stayed for two.

I bumped into two girls who knew me. I had no idea at all who they were. They were both pregnant. They asked me what I was up to now. I didn't tell them about you. They looked at me expecting me to comment about their baby to or ask them about their baby or anything like that but I didn't and their disapproval at my inappropriate neglect was written all over their faces.

We're all born. We all die. It's nothing. It's not worth commenting on.

I'll tell you what I hadn't expected. I hadn't expected Anka's smile.

She saw me, she bounded up to me. Really ran. Across the house. Jumped into my arms.

'Uncle Willem!'

I honestly have no idea what I did to deserve a greeting like that. I barely talked to her yesterday.

She wanted me to play in the snow with her. I told her I hate snow, which I do. I can never move properly in the snow. But I did go outside with her and I did play with her for a while. I was very bad at playing with her. We made a very bad snowman that was smaller than she wanted it to be because I didn't want to stay outside for too long.

And she threw a few snowballs at me that didn't hit me even though I stood completely still and she was about three metres away.

We had the soup and the soup was fine and Mum roasted a chicken and it was great. And I'll tell you, I'll say this. It reminded me of home. That taste. I mean I know people always say that and I know also that chicken as a meat is sold all over the world and doesn't taste that different, not really. But there was something about the taste of Mum's chicken that did make me think that nobody cooks chicken like her. I'm lying to myself. Millions and millions of people cook chicken exactly like her. Of course they do.

After we'd eaten there was a moment when everybody was sitting round the table, me and Dad and Mum and Henrick and Uncle Michiel and Mina, not Anka, I don't think Anka, but everybody else was looking at different things on their iPhones. We sat in silence. I didn't ask anybody else what they were looking at. We were all thinking about you on some level, I suppose.

I was washing up after dinner when Dad came in. He asked me if I was staying at the Lloyd again tonight. I told him I was. He nodded. He said that was probably for the best.

I asked him why.

'I know you never liked Pauli. The way you talked about him when you were children. And when he got older all he wanted was for you to ask him to go and see you and stay with you for a while. Of course you didn't. But he was your brother, Willem. You come back home. You won't stay at the house. You go to the funeral. You stare at everybody. You don't even try to look sad.'

Mum called for us. She interrupted him.

Uncle Michiel and Henrick and Anka had decided they would do a firework display for you. Uncle Michiel brought some fireworks with him from a man he knew who'd got them from China. There were rockets and catherine wheels and Anka got a sparkler. Mina tried to take it off her, she said it was dangerous, but everybody told her to stop being so silly and Uncle Michiel lit Anka's sparkler for her. She danced around the garden. She was writing her name in the air. Over and over. I asked her to write my name and she wouldn't. Mum asked her to write your name and she got a bit confused but Mum kind of forced her to write your name and she did. She did it really well. She was laughing at me. She kept telling me my face was funny when I was watching her write names in sparks in the night.

It was amazing watching her. She had no idea how much sadness she was going to experience in her life. She had no understanding of the idea of regret. She'd never drunk herself to sleep. She'd never deliberately hurt a person she loved just to see if she could. She had no idea how much uncertainty she would feel one day. She had no idea what was going to happen to the world when the money runs out, and it will, and the water runs out, and it will, and the antibiotics stop working and the oxygen thins and the terrorists in terror groups all over the world have got so bored of economies that leave them scapegoated and desperate that we may as well package them and market them and monetise them to the hilt and then gather them together and blow them all to pieces. Because it's clearly not working, Pauli, it's not, it's just not, it's done, we're done, it's over.

I whispered to Anka not to tell anybody but I was going back to my hotel. I asked her to keep it to herself.

I walked back. Down the Herengracht. The snow on the canal made everything feel silent. When you work with numbers you spend a lot of your life working from the idea that some things don't change. I watched the snow melt on the canal and realised this was wrong. Death makes numbers less definite.

I wish I'd been with you when you died.

I don't really.

I don't think I could have faced it. I would have told you not to be so hysterical. I wouldn't have been able to stop laughing.

January 30th

Dear Pauli

I met Isaac this morning. We went to a café in the middle of Prinsengracht.

It was his favourite café, he said. I think he wanted to go there because he knew everybody. It was so beautifully light it made me want to be sick. I almost put my sunglasses on. There was nothing covert about meeting me there. It was like he was bringing me here to show me just how happy his life had become.

He hasn't changed. The least he could have done was get a bit fat. I told him. He looked at me like I'd told him a joke he didn't understand.

I ordered a bottle of white wine. He had a glass but it barely touched his lips.

He's working restoring canal boats. When he told me that I thought he was joking. He wasn't.

His favourite is when people bring him antique boats. He restores the paint. He looks after the engine.

He likes it because he's bringing something back to life. The older the boat, the more damaged it is, the better.

I nodded. As though I really understood.

He asked me what my job was. I told him I bought things and sold them again. He asked me what kind of things. I said countries. I was kind of joking. More like cities than countries.

He asked me about New York. Is it very different to Amsterdam?

I told him it was exactly the same. New York *is* Amsterdam.

The land's different. The granite. That's all. It means people can build bigger buildings there. Apart from that it's exactly the same. I told him in downtown New York there were artifacts from Amsterdam from the Golden Age.

In the foundations of skyscrapers there are fossils of farm animals and cherry trees and clay pipes brought over by Dutch explorers in the seventeenth century.

I wonder if people noticed, he said to me, that they were living in a Golden Age. Or do you only ever realise you're living through a Golden Age after it's gone?

It was when he said that to me that I reached over to the table and touched his cheek.

I wanted to tell him: you are the only person left on earth who I think is in any way sane; you are the person I've been waiting to speak to for fourteen years; you make me feel like a child; you make me want to lie down on the floor; you make me want to empty your dishwasher; you make me want to insist you go to the dentist regularly and buy you fresh fruit smoothies and hold your hand in supermarkets and remember to record your favourite programmes on TV; you make everything that is rational in my world, and my world is very rational, you make all of that seem magical and strange and full of poetry and I hate it because I can't talk to anybody like this and I want to, I want to, I try, I want to. I've missed you. Fuck I've missed you. I've thought about you every day. I so have. I have.

> *Come home traveller, come home*
> *That's the tired old poem*
> *Your heart keeps singing*
> *There's no lock, there's no key*
> *What makes us free*
> *It's what you're leaving*

I didn't say that. I retracted my hand straight away. I shouldn't have touched him at all. I said to him:

'Do you want to come back to my room? You could if you wanted to.'

He had no idea I was going to say that. He wouldn't have come to meet me if he'd thought I was going to do that. He had no idea I thought about him. He never thought about me. Not like that. I hadn't crossed his mind for years, for years. Not until I'd texted him to tell him about you.

Twelve years ago I walked out on him because I thought it wasn't working. I had this notion about how I was meant to be feeling and our relationship didn't fit into this notion at all and sometimes it's better to control these things. Isaac said it was fine now. He's much happier now. He looked all around him at the people in the café as though he was embarrassed these people had seen what I'd done.

I found to my surprise I was shaking like a leaf. I found it suddenly very difficult to talk. I blinked my hardest to stop myself from crying but I couldn't. I found to my surprise, real tears pouring down my face.

'I'm sorry. I'm being silly. It's not you. Honestly.'

We didn't swap emails. In case you were wondering. We shook hands. He tried to give me a hug but I don't really know how to hug anybody any more. I just stood there. Staring. I felt stupid.

I walked to Mum and Dad's house.

Mum and Dad were surprised to see me. They invited me in for lunch. I helped Mum make some chicken salad with the left-over chicken and we all ate that and I took some bags of rubbish out of the flat. I thought they were from the party but she told me to go and look in your room.

Everything was cleared away. Your posters were gone and your clothes were gone. Your records and your books were gone. She'd stayed up all night and cleared out your room.

Most of it was in boxes. In the basement of the apartment. The rubbish bags were just bits of paper she'd sorted through.

She said she knew people weren't meant to do things like this.
You hear stories of mothers whose children have died and
they keep their bedrooms the same, they don't touch them,
they turn them into a shrine. She didn't want to be one of
those mothers.

She asked if I wanted your guitar. I can't play it. It would cost
a lot of money to ship it over.

I asked Mum if I should stay for dinner and she told me I
shouldn't. She looked right at me. She said it was time for me
to go home.

Dad had to go and get some vegetables. I told him I'd walk
with him.

I gave Mum a hug and went to say goodbye to her. She burst
out crying. She cried and cried into my chest. Big whole
shaking tears. Her face was soaking wet. It felt like the
appropriate thing would be to cry with her but I couldn't.
It wasn't my place to cry. My sadness was nothing compared
to hers. I don't know how long she held on to me. Dad stood
there. Watching. He said 'There, there. There, there.'

I walked with him to the corner of the street where he turned
to get the vegetables. We shook hands and did a very bad
hug. I told him I was sorry you'd died. He nodded. We didn't
say anything about the things he said to me last night.

I stood watching as he walked around the corner and walked
away.

Written down in the sand
Or in your lover's hand
That's your life story
No matter what you fear
It's where you disappear
That's the mystery
Go where the love is
Where the love is go

You told me once that talking was just a peculiar form of
breathing. It was like posh breathing for humans, you said.

And that singing was something deeper and richer and stranger and more incredible. You told me that scientists had started to think, when they studied the vocal cords of the earliest human beings, that hunter-gatherers sung before they spoke. They didn't live so close together. There weren't so many of them. They needed to communicate over long distances.

So we are animals born to sing more than we're animals born to talk. It sounded unlikely, to me. But I liked the way you said it.

January 31st

Dear Pauli

Mina picked me up at about six-thirty. The kids were very excited to see me. I was too tired for their excitement.

Anka wanted to sit next to me in the car. I wanted to sit next to her too.

Mina told me to sit in the front seat so I did.

Anka asked me when I was next coming home. I told her I didn't know. Probably not for a long time. She'd be an adult or something. She looked confused. Like she couldn't tell if I was joking or not but she was used to that in grown-ups.

Mina said to me that she was worried about me. I'd been behaving really oddly and I'd really upset Mum and Dad. She said it was like I didn't even try to look after them. And I didn't say anything to anybody for the whole trip. I was just really weird with them both and with Anka and was I all right? I should hear the way Mum and Dad talk about me when I'm not there. They talk about me all the time. She's not like me, she said. She has to keep things under control and keep things clean and work, really hard sometimes. I don't need to do that. But that was no reason to behave the way I did, because, she said, frankly if she didn't know me better she'd say I was being a fucking prick.

She said this really quietly so the children couldn't hear her swearing.

'Are you sure you're all right, Willem? You can tell me.' I told her I was completely fine. She looked at me.

Just because something's not perfect doesn't mean you should just walk away from it, Willem, you stupid fuck.

I looked at her without saying a word. It seemed to last for hours.

She leant in. She gave me a very, very gentle hug and she was breathing slowly. I loved feeling her standing against me trying to control her breath.

I watched them drive away. Waved goodbye. But my wave was really pathetic. It was this little shit wave. They couldn't have seen it.

What's funny is that I saw you. After I checked in and checked my bags in and got through security and headed to the departures I went back to Murphy's Bar, opened another packet of American Spirit and ordered a double Scotch and ginger.

I should stop drinking. I'm drinking so much these days. It's too much, I know that.

But I did. I saw you in the bar.

You were sitting on your own. Of course you were. Your feet up on the sofa. You were listening to your iPod. You were nodding your head in time to the music. Ever so gently so you didn't draw attention to yourself.

You looked right at me. You didn't smile. I'm not even sure you saw me. Did you see me, Pauli?

You looked like you were looking into the middle distance.

Your hair's changed colour. Maybe that happens after you die. It might be. And you were fatter, a little bit fatter than you were and that was surprising. But it was definitely you.

I wanted to go over. Give you a hug. Tell you how happy I was to see you. Say, is this what happens now? Do I just keep bumping into you now at airport bars and places like that? Is this what happens when people die?

I didn't do anything.

> *Go where the love is*
> *Where the love is go*
> *Give away your good name*
> *Your pride and shame*
> *Or you won't get far*
> *Don't get lost and fall in a trap*
> *Don't need a map*
> *Or to follow a star*
> *Go where the love is*
> *Where the love is go*
> *Go where the love is*
> *Where the love is go*
> *It's not where you are*
> *It's where you disappear*
> *Is there someone near*
> *To wish goodbye*

I just finished my drink. Checked my passport. Checked my boarding pass.

I wondered, briefly, what on earth I'm going to do with all these letters. I honestly have no idea. And I've no idea when I'm going to stop writing them. I will. I will. I mean of course I will.

I headed to the departure gate. It was time.

Go Where the Love Is (Song from Far Away)

Mark Eitzel

 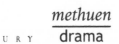

Bloomsbury Methuen Drama Modern Plays
include work by

Bola Agbaje
Edward Albee
Davey Anderson
Jean Anouilh
John Arden
Peter Barnes
Sebastian Barry
Alistair Beaton
Brendan Behan
Edward Bond
William Boyd
Bertolt Brecht
Howard Brenton
Amelia Bullmore
Anthony Burgess
Leo Butler
Jim Cartwright
Lolita Chakrabarti
Caryl Churchill
Lucinda Coxon
Curious Directive
Nick Darke
Shelagh Delaney
Ishy Din
Claire Dowie
David Edgar
David Eldridge
Dario Fo
Michael Frayn
John Godber
Paul Godfrey
James Graham
David Greig
John Guare
Mark Haddon
Peter Handke
David Harrower
Jonathan Harvey
Iain Heggie

Robert Holman
Caroline Horton
Terry Johnson
Sarah Kane
Barrie Keeffe
Doug Lucie
Anders Lustgarten
David Mamet
Patrick Marber
Martin McDonagh
Arthur Miller
D. C. Moore
Tom Murphy
Phyllis Nagy
Anthony Neilson
Peter Nichols
Joe Orton
Joe Penhall
Luigi Pirandello
Stephen Poliakoff
Lucy Prebble
Peter Quilter
Mark Ravenhill
Philip Ridley
Willy Russell
Jean-Paul Sartre
Sam Shepard
Martin Sherman
Wole Soyinka
Simon Stephens
Peter Straughan
Kate Tempest
Theatre Workshop
Judy Upton
Timberlake Wertenbaker
Roy Williams
Snoo Wilson
Frances Ya-Chu Cowhig
Benjamin Zephaniah

Bloomsbury Methuen Drama Contemporary Dramatists
include

John Arden (two volumes)
Arden & D'Arcy
Peter Barnes (three volumes)
Sebastian Barry
Mike Bartlett
Dermot Bolger
Edward Bond (eight volumes)
Howard Brenton (two volumes)
Leo Butler
Richard Cameron
Jim Cartwright
Caryl Churchill (two volumes)
Complicite
Sarah Daniels (two volumes)
Nick Darke
David Edgar (three volumes)
David Eldridge (two volumes)
Ben Elton
Per Olov Enquist
Dario Fo (two volumes)
Michael Frayn (four volumes)
John Godber (four volumes)
Paul Godfrey
James Graham
David Greig
John Guare
Lee Hall (two volumes)
Katori Hall
Peter Handke
Jonathan Harvey (two volumes)
Iain Heggie
Israel Horovitz
Declan Hughes
Terry Johnson (three volumes)
Sarah Kane
Barrie Keeffe
Bernard-Marie Koltès (two volumes)
Franz Xaver Kroetz
Kwame Kwei-Armah
David Lan
Bryony Lavery
Deborah Levy
Doug Lucie

David Mamet (four volumes)
Patrick Marber
Martin McDonagh
Duncan McLean
David Mercer (two volumes)
Anthony Minghella (two volumes)
Tom Murphy (six volumes)
Phyllis Nagy
Anthony Neilson (two volumes)
Peter Nichol (two volumes)
Philip Osment
Gary Owen
Louise Page
Stewart Parker (two volumes)
Joe Penhall (two volumes)
Stephen Poliakoff (three volumes)
David Rabe (two volumes)
Mark Ravenhill (three volumes)
Christina Reid
Philip Ridley (two volumes)
Willy Russell
Eric-Emmanuel Schmitt
Ntozake Shange
Sam Shepard (two volumes)
Martin Sherman (two volumes)
Christopher Shinn
Joshua Sobel
Wole Soyinka (two volumes)
Simon Stephens (three volumes)
Shelagh Stephenson
David Storey (three volumes)
C. P. Taylor
Sue Townsend
Judy Upton
Michel Vinaver (two volumes)
Arnold Wesker (two volumes)
Peter Whelan
Michael Wilcox
Roy Williams (four volumes)
David Williamson
Snoo Wilson (two volumes)
David Wood (two volumes)
Victoria Wood

For a complete catalogue
of Bloomsbury Methuen Drama
titles write to:

Bloomsbury Methuen Drama
Bloomsbury Publishing Plc
50 Bedford Square
London WC1B 3DP

or you can visit our website at:
www.bloomsbury.com/drama